# AND HE SAID, "PRAISE ME!"

All for His Glory!
Penny Meyer Hovda

PENNY MEYER HOVDA

**AND HE SAID, PRAISE ME!**



Library of Congress Control Number: 2017949611

| ISBN-13: | Paperback: | 978-1-64045-293-0 |
|---|---|---|
| | PDF: | 978-1-64045-294-7 |
| | ePub: | 978-1-64045-295-4 |
| | Kindle: | 978-1-64045-296-1 |

Printed in the United States of America

LitFire LLC
1-800-511-9787
www.litfirepublishing.com
order@litfirepublishing.com

FOREWORD 9
PREFACE 11
NOVEMBER 25, 2005 13
THE CROSS 17
MY STRENGTH 21
CATCH AND RELEASE 25
EARTH ANGELS 29
LIFTED UP 33
PRAYERFUL PRAISE 37
FREEDOM 41
HAIR CARES 45
JUST BREATHE 49
PASS IT ON 53
WHITE HORSES 57
EPILOGUE 61
"LETTER FROM HEAVEN" 67
A SALVATION PRAYER 69

## PRAISES FOR: **AND HE SAID, "PRAISE ME!"**

--Pastor John Snyder, Crossroads Community Church, Parker, Colorado writes:

In her pain, God spoke comfort and strength to Penny's Heart. In her healing, Penny writes from her heart to us...*And He Said, "Praise Me"* is from her heart and will inspire and encourage any who will make the time to read it!

---Linda Evans Shepherd, author of *When You Don't Know What to Pray* and *The Potluck Club* novels and host of WebTV4Women.tv., writes:

Penny Hovda has captured my heart as she captured her heart's journey that brought her through incredible loss then to incredible joy and intimacy with God. What an encouraging word!

---Melody Pew writes:

*"And He said, Praise Me!"* is more than the author's walk through breast cancer. It is a powerful story of her spiritual walk as she takes us with her on her personal journey of hearing His voice, trusting in His word and obeying His commands. It made me laugh, it made me cry, it gave me hope.

---Laura Bracklien writes:

God has brought "...beauty for ashes; the oil instead of mourning and a garment of praise instead of a spirit of despair." Thank you for letting Him use you and your tribulation to bless so many.

---Joe Lewis, musician/recording artist-album: *The Joe Lewis Band,* writes:

I look forward to reading the new version as the other blessed me so...you are a good writer. I felt I was right there reading the book. You have the ability to take the reader to another place.

Jill Weisenberger forwarded this message from a friend going through breast cancer:

*"I just wanted to say thanks for the book and thinking of me during one of the scariest times of my life. I read the book about a week after my first surgery and I cried throughout the entire time I was reading it! It was crazy as I could have written that book. It was me to a tee! God works in amazing ways and I believe you sharing this book with me was one of them."*

AND HE SAID,

# "Praise Me!"

*An Inspirational Reflection of One Women's Journey Through Breast Cancer*

# AND HE SAID, "Praise Me!"

PENNY MEYER HOVDA

***You have vindicated me; you have endorsed my work, declaring from your throne that it is good.***

***-Psalm 9:4 (TLB)***

(The moment the publishing company asked me about endorsements for my book, God gave me this scripture. If I had no other accolades to this book, this one would be enough.)

# DEDICATION

To the One who inspired me to write it:
My Lord and Savior, Jesus Christ

It was after my 18 month long battle when God told me, "*Now write what you went searching for.*" So I did.

# ACKNOWLEDGMENTS


I would like to thank my loving husband, Tim, whose quiet strength offered solace in the journey of my self-sacrifice, examination, and spiritual awakening.

To my daughter, Lindsay, for which my cup and saucer overflow with the gift of laughter and friendship you bring to my heart and soul every day—Thank you!

To my loving sisters, Ilo and Kim. Thank you for being there and for lifting my spirit with your words of encouragement and so much more daily.

To my mom. Words cannot begin to tell you how thankful I am for your expression of love and concern for me in my time of need. You reflect God's love with your giving spirit and continual service to Him. I love you so much!

To my friend, Elaine. You are my inspiration! This experience would have taken a much different path had I not known you. Your faith and positive attitude in the face of adversity reminds me how God uses us in the work He is doing to bring glory and honor to His name. Thank you for reminding me to always be thankful, even when I am walking in the valleys.

To Nicole. I can't tell you how much you touched my heart with all the cards you sent. Every day, I would get a new card in the mail from you. Thank you so much for your encouragement and prayers and the food you provided.

To Jared and Lance. Thank you so much for all you've done. Your generosity will never be forgotten.

To Ilo and Dean. Thank you for sharing your gifts in order to bring this book to fruition. I am moved by your generosity and sense of humility in which it was given.

To BJ, my friend. Thank You so much for your help in making this book become a reality. You helped me see the vision for my book even before it was written.

To Jenny Chan LaRoux. Thank you for everything you did with the marketing of this book. God places people in your life to help in areas you need and He brought me you!

Finally, I would like to thank the communities of believers who were praying for me. Your prayers wrapped me like a blanket that kept me warm and secure in His loving arms. Even when I couldn't seem to pray myself, I felt those prayers. His protection and strength were given as He held me in the palm of His hand at a time when I needed it most.

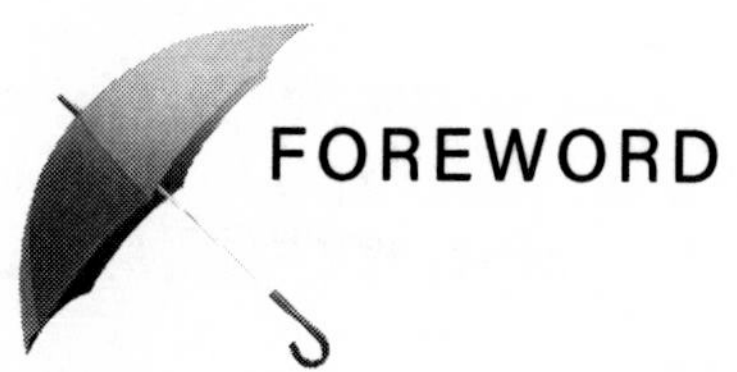

# FOREWORD

Penny Hovda taught me how to do cancer way before I knew I would need it. Shortly after Penny's experience, my husband was diagnosed with throat cancer, and as we both learned, cancer affects the entire family, not just the person who has it.

Penny's graceful way of accepting her fate, continuing her life with a smile, and constantly praising God was beautiful to watch. She was an inspiration way before cancer visited my home.

Because of Penny's example, we were able to accept what had to be done and to praise God in the process. We never gave up, and with the love of our church family and encouragement from people in our lives like Penny, we too are now cancer survivors. `

*And He Said, "Praise Me!"* is not just another book about cancer. It is a book about surviving the unexpected, overwhelming, inopportune catastrophes that life throws our way. Penny shares the ways that she found God through her journey, from jet contrails to sticky-lint rollers.

Throughout our friendship, Penny has helped me face my battles by utilizing the strength of God. From beginning to end, *And He Said, "Praise Me"* will challenge, encourage, and inspire you to face your struggles by releasing them into God's able hands.

This is a book that you will refer back to many times over your life. And when you do, it will help you find God and praise him regardless of your circumstances. May God bless you always! Never forget: He's always there, but it's up to you to allow Him in.

-BJ Cosper

*I will be glad and rejoice in your love, for you saw my affliction and knew the anguish of my soul. You have not handed me over to the enemy but have set my feet in a spacious place.*

-Psalm 31:7-8

# PREFACE

I wrote this book in order that others may be blessed, transformed, and renewed in the midst of their unexpected tragedy, illness, and devastation. I found my Comforter, Counselor, and Friend above all Friends to be my Lord and Savior, Jesus Christ. It was during the lowest time of my life that He spoke to me. What He told me seemed incomprehensible in my state of mind. To tell me to praise Him for my cancer was to accept this event in my life and celebrate it. As you could imagine, that was the last thing I thought of or felt like doing. However, what I began to realize is when we offer up our sacrificial praise, God's love and ever-present Spirit becomes evident in the trials we face. Putting aside your feelings and obediently doing what He says can change the course of the journey you are traveling. Our reverence of praise should not only be offered up when things are well with us, but in all things, good or bad. I have learned that through trust and obedience to Him, He will turn our tragedies to triumph and our sorrows to blessings. So whatever giant you are facing, be reminded that there is none greater, bigger, or stronger than our God. He will take on your challenge and help you overcome that which seems insurmountable. You will see the evidence of His hand at work in yours, and your victory will not be just surviving but knowing that the true reward is living beyond yourself in relationship with Him, through Him, and in Him.

*Therefore by Him, let us continually offer the sacrifice of praise to God, that is, the fruit of our lips, giving thanks to His name.*

-Hebrews 13: 15 (NKJV)

# NOVEMBER 25, 2005

I was sitting in the car. My daughter was with me. We had just picked up a few things from a local retail store as a means to pass the time. We made small talk even though we both knew what was on each other's mind. The nurse told me to call if I hadn't heard by 2:00 today. It was now 2:10. I told myself that no news was good news, but I felt myself becoming more and more worried as each minute passed. *Why do they make you wait like this I thought? This is my life we are talking about!* Finally, we decided that I needed to make the call. I was glad I wasn't alone. The nurse apologized for not contacting me. She said she thought the doctor would have called me by now. I knew then what she was about to say, but she didn't want to be the one to tell me. It was cancer, DCIS, or rather, ductile carcinoma in-situ. The biopsy confirmed it. She tried to explain it, but my head was spinning. I was hardly able to listen because my mind was still hanging onto those first words. Then I heard doctors, surgeons, names…what? Did I need referrals? Hold on. What? *It can't be,* I thought. "Yes, please," was my reply as I searched for a pen and paper to write the names and numbers I would have to call. Then she said she was sorry and, "Good luck to you."

I looked over at Lindsay. My fear was all over her face. Disbelief and confusion were all I remember feeling—and the strong sense that I had to call my mom. I really needed to talk to my mom. She, better than anyone, would know what to say to make me feel better, or maybe it was just that I needed the comfort of her words since she wasn't here to hold me. That call was not an easy one to make, but my mother, as I knew she would, immediately had me on the community prayer chains and was booking her ticket to come and be with me. So this is how it all started. Little did I know how much my life was about to change and the impact it would have on me and my family.

*I will lead the blind by ways they have not known, along unfamiliar paths I will guide them; I will turn the darkness into light before them and make the rough places smooth. These are the things I will do; I will not forsake them.*

-Isaiah 42:16 (NIV)

# Your Story

## Your Story

# THE CROSS

I'll never forget the Sunday after my diagnosis, just two days earlier. On our way to church, my daughter and I both looked with amazement at the enormous, cross-shaped contrails that filled the sky. To me, it was as if God was telling me He was with me and to keep my eyes on Him. Ever since, that cross has been imprinted on my brain. What I didn't realize until later was the exact likeness of that cross to the one that adorns the cover of our church bulletin and the Crossroads Community Church sign on top of the hill. You see, I have no doubt God brought me to this place just a few months earlier, knowing it would serve as the "well" from which I would draw my inspiration and strength. This Sunday was no different. I remember feeling the uncertainty of the months ahead. Looking back, I'm glad I didn't know all that was to take place over the next eighteen months. I think we are blessed with not knowing our futures. It's the only way to truly put yourself in God's hands when you feel so utterly captured with life's uncertainty.

It was the Thanksgiving service at church. I had no idea what that meant at the time, but quickly, I learned it was a so-called "open mic" service, where anyone could speak, share a need or a praise...whatever God put on their hearts to share. I remember being too scared to share in front of so many people but wanted so badly to ask for a prayer of healing. Instead, I listened. God knew that by me listening to others share of their struggles and physical ailments, I would no longer be focused on me but on them. I realized that day I wasn't alone in my suffering. Isn't there a saying, "Misery loves company?" Well, it's true! I felt better! In fact, I remember thanking God that all I had was cancer! I realized then and there that I wouldn't trade my problem with any of theirs. I left that service knowing God allows things to happen in our lives for a reason, and soon I would begin to learn what that reason was. In the meantime, I felt comforted knowing He was in control and I was just along for the ride.

*The Lord is my shepherd; I shall not be in want. He makes me lie down in green pastures, he leads me beside quiet waters, he restores my soul. He guides me in paths of righteousness for his name's sake. Even though I walk through the valley of the shadow of death, I will fear no evil, for you are with me; your rod and your staff, they comfort me. You prepare a table before me in the presence of my enemies. You anoint my head with oil; my cup overflows. Surely goodness and love will follow me all the days of my life, and I will dwell in the house of the Lord forever.*

-Psalm 23 (NIV)

# Your Story

# Your Story

# MY STRENGTH

*My grace is sufficient for you, for my strength is made perfect in weakness. Therefore most gladly I will rather boast in my infirmities that the power of Christ may rest upon me.*

-2 Corinthians 12:9(NIV)

God speaks to us in many ways. This verse in 2 Corinthians came to me when I was wrought with fatigue. Many days I wondered if I was going to have enough strength to work the next day. Doing any daily activity at all was draining. It hurt just to think. Time and time again, I would recall this verse, and it reassured me that I needn't worry about the next day, hour, or minute. He had me covered. I claimed this verse on my life when I felt the fatigue was going to overtake me. It never did, and I never let myself succumb to its incapacity. Instead, God covered me with His strength. That season of my life has passed now, but when I reflect on those days, I am still overwhelmed. I found that God meets our needs when we need Him and in what sense we need Him. All we need to do is ask, trust, and obey. Obedience is allowing Him to give you what He wants for you at the time you ask and believing in your heart that it will be so. You need to trust and let go and then let God catch you where you fall. He will pull you up, hold you, and carry you as long as you need. I would imagine myself clinging onto a cliff, my hands starting to slip until I was hanging on by my fingertips alone. Just when I couldn't hold on any more, God's long reach would grasp my wrists firmly to lift me up.

Our wills are so strong that it takes all we have to give it up, but when we do, finally, His power and His grace and His strength are given. It is getting easier for me to let go. It takes practice, but more and more, I'm learning to stop trying to scale these mountains alone. Instead, I will plant my feet on His firm foundation, and my hands will be doing nothing but reaching out to His.

*I can do everything through him who gives me strength.*

-Philippians 4:13 (NIV)

# Your Story

# Your Story

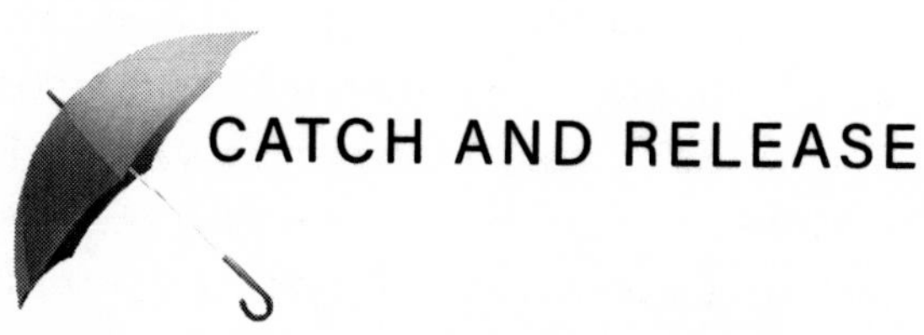

# CATCH AND RELEASE

Day by day, I am reminded of how precious our time on earth is. More and more, my eyes are opened to see and experience God's creation around me.

Sometimes, we can lose our perspective and slip into a pattern of complacency. The world has a way of weaving a web that can trap us into believing we can do anything apart from God. That's the place I was at the time of my diagnosis. Then God caught me—my attention that is. He allowed this attack on my body, and I was brought to my knees. It was long overdue. God wanted to bring me back into a love relationship with Him, but I didn't read the signs. It took something drastic like cancer to help me see what really mattered. I compare it to fishing, and the hook that snagged me was cancer.

God tells us we need to die unto ourselves in order that we may live. Even though the cancer and the treatments did not kill me, my body's immune system plummeted. This was necessary in order for my body to start the recovery and rebuilding process. I believe we need to go through the valleys in order to appreciate the view from the mountaintops. It has certainly changed my perspective, and it is comforting to know that we are always connected to our heavenly Father. He may let out the line to give us some play, but if we take it too far, He will pull us back, sometimes hard, and other times only a gentle tug is enough. We may struggle and pull back, but when we release our will to His, His gentleness and love always leads us to restoration and a renewal of mind, body, and spirit.

I wanted to quit my treatments. My will was fighting the sickening effects of the chemotherapy. This went against the advice of my doctor, who very sternly reminded me of the aggressive state of my cancer. He said he'd like to see me around in ten years. I was made to realize that he too was only looking out for my best interests. So, I followed through and fought the fight and came out ahead. Instead of fighting the treatments, I fought the disease. I learned to listen to God and my doctor. That changed the course of everything. Yes, I still had to suffer through the effects of the chemo and the surgeries, but I allowed God to carry me, guide me, restore His spirit in me, and bless me beyond measure. His deliverance through my cancer brought restoration of a relationship with Him that was long past due.

Now, when I feel God tugging on the line between us, I am reminded to release my will to His in order to freely experience Him in my life. I feel comforted knowing that, even when I tug back, that line will never break. He's always there to reel me in a little closer, and when He does, I'm blessed.

*I am the vine; you are the branches. If a man remains in me and I in him, he will bear much fruit; apart from me you can do nothing.*

-John 15:5 (NIV)

# Your Story

# Your Story

# EARTH ANGELS

All throughout my journey with breast cancer, there were many strangers I met who touched my life and my heart. These so-called strangers were like ministering angels who lifted me, shared with me, cried with me, gave me hope, and left me changed. Even though I saw them briefly, their impressions will always be with me.

I remember grocery shopping when a gentleman handed me a small, gold foil angel. He said, "I thought you could use an angel in your pocket." You see, my bald head made it obvious to him that I was sick. I smiled and thanked him as he placed this angel in the palm of my hand. It touched my heart that he cared enough to show me he cared. I would be reminded of this encounter often because that little gold foil angel would somehow be discovered time and time again. This was because I would unintentionally lose it and then find it, and then lose it and find it again and again.

Then there was a woman named Peggy with whom I stood in line waiting to vote for three hours. After one hour, we finally made introductions, which led to small talk, which led to conversation, and then a realization of the common bond we shared. She too was a breast cancer survivor.

Another was a woman walking right beside me in the store. I looked at her at the same time she looked at me. We laughed.

We were both wearing pink t-shirts and sporting pink hats on bald heads. We exchanged our stories and hugged. I don't remember her name, but I smile every time I recall that moment.

There are many more fond memories to look back on, and some would question these as chance encounters, but to me, I believe they were God's ministering angels. Whether they were regular people like you and I or heaven sent, they did something. That something was just what I needed at that time and in that moment to get me from there to here. Those ministering spirits, like angels, are all of us reaching out to others in need as we are called upon according to His purpose. We need to be reminded what God tells us in Hebrews 13:2 (NIV): "Do not forget to entertain strangers, for by so doing some people have entertained angels without knowing it."

*Are not all angels ministering spirits sent to serve those who will inherit salvation?*

-Hebrews 1:14 (NIV)

# Your Story

# Your Story

# LIFTED UP

Inspiration comes in many forms. Mine came from love, so much love that to give up would be letting down all those He had fighting for me. I had literally communities of believers praying for me. Even when I couldn't pray for myself, I felt "lifted up." So many people—some I hadn't spoken to or thought of for years—yet they called, prayed, or sent cards. So many people cared enough to reach out, lift up, show up, shut up, speak up, listen, or just be.

My heroes, of course, are those who suffered with me, like my devoted husband. He never showed me how scared he really was, yet he gave me his shoulders anytime I needed them to cry on. Then there's my beautiful daughter, Lindsay. She was my warrior. I know inside she was like a scared kitten, but to me, she was as brave as a lioness protecting her own. My mom was my rescuer. She did things for me that only a mother could so willingly and lovingly do. My sisters, my best friends—I can't imagine my life without them and theirs without mine. I know this crossed their minds, yet never a word was spoken that wasn't to strengthen, inspire, or empower me in believing that I was above this, that I could do anything I put my mind to, even fighting cancer.

My friend, Elaine; her inspirational journey as a breast cancer overcomer was a big influence on how I faced my foe.

Only four years earlier, she ran the race I was just beginning. At the time, I remember thinking, *She is the bravest and strongest person I know.* I didn't know at the time I'd be put to the challenge of my own resolutions.

And then there were my prayer sisters, or should I say my prayer warriors; I would not have had the strength to carry on without them. Each week, we would pray, and oh how amazing is the power of prayer when two or more are gathered! His strength is made perfect in our weakness, as the scriptures say, and it was His strength alone that got me through week after week working full-time when I felt like all I wanted to do was sleep. These wonderful ladies were my cheerleaders. They carried me when I couldn't go on and continue to honor me with their friendship.

There is a quote by John Chariton Collins which reads, "In prosperity our friends know us; in adversity we know our friends." Having lived through adversity, I know this to be true now more than ever. The reaction from one I regarded as "close" left me with feelings of abandonment. A different kind of hurt, yes, but whose harbor finally led to release through forgiveness. Even though I may never understand what happened, the emptiness I once felt from a relationship lost has now been filled. My cup and saucer overflow with praise and thanksgiving to Him who gave me life a second time.

*Blessed is he who has regard for the weak; the Lord delivers him in times of trouble. The Lord will protect him and preserve his life; He will bless him in the land and not surrender him to the desire of his foes. The Lord will sustain him on his sickbed and restore him from his bed of illness.*

-Psalm 41:1-3 (NIV)

# Your Story

# Your Story

# PRAYERFUL PRAISE

There are many emotions a person deals with after a trauma. It may be an accident; death of a loved one; or, in my case, a cancer diagnosis. I remember feelings of denial, anger, and pity and, finally, acceptance, defiance, and hope. A pivotal event of this whole journey occurred as I laid awake thinking and praying. I remember asking God what I was supposed to do and how I was to feel. I knew I was angry, but there was no one to blame for my illness. I cried out to God. His reply changed my outlook on the journey I was about to travel.

He said, "*Praise Me*"! It was the last thing I felt or thought of doing. In fact, I hadn't even been able to pray—not really anyway. The words were empty, so I quit for a time. Instead, I found myself asking Him questions out loud and talking to Him like He was in the room with me. Our relationship had changed. It became personal. I felt Him with me like never before. I knew He had always been there, but I didn't involve myself in His works. So what was different? God had my attention. Until then, I had become very complacent in my spirituality. What recourse did I have other than to hit my knees and beg for mercy? Did I cause this to happen? I know I didn't exercise enough, eat well enough, sleep enough, or pray enough. It took being faced with my own mortality to bring about the changes I needed to heal both physically and spiritually. So, each day, in my thankfulness,

He blessed me. My eyes were opened wide to His intervention in the midst of all the unpleasantries from the treatments, biopsies, and surgeries. You see, despite our circumstances, the God of the universe deserves to be praised. And when you praise Him sacrificially out of your hurt and pain, He will bless you.

Looking back, I see a lot of tears, but more than that were tears of triumph, an abundance of love and support from family and friends; and most importantly, God's ever-present Spirit. His Word says we are to pray continually, giving thanks in all circumstances. I know there will be more trials ahead, but I also know that God is in control of everything. He will bring about good in any circumstance.

One thing I have learned is to not take advantage of each other, our freedoms, or our lives here on earth. Every day is truly a gift from God. And when we discipline ourselves to see the good things, be it in one another, nature, or life in general, we begin to look outside of ourselves to the very heart of God because He is everywhere and in everything. It may be harder to see Him under a veil of darkness and despair, but He is omniscient (all-knowing) and omnipotent (all-powerful). So give thanks and be blessed by the One who loves you as far as the east is from the west, and know that how you respond to that love is directly related to your relationship with Him.

*Be joyful always; pray continually; give thanks in all circumstances, for this is God's will for you in Christ Jesus.*

-1 Thessalonians 5:16-18 (NIV)

# *Your Story*

# Your Story

# FREEDOM

There are many ways we know and feel and live freedom. But to truly be free from within ourselves the way God created us to be is something only He can make happen. I'm not talking about the transformation of our hearts when we ask Him into our lives, although this is necessary in order to take the next step.

Going through cancer helped me see me—not the one I see in the mirror but the true me from within myself. Let me explain. I gave up control of my life. I gave up my hair, my eyebrows, and my eyelashes. I gave up my breasts. And, visually and prayerfully, I laid myself at the feet of Jesus. I asked Him to show me myself as He saw me because I didn't recognize the woman looking back at me in the mirror. *I felt unlovely.*

God began to show me the real me from the inside out—no wigs, no makeup, no cover. And, you know, we live in a secular world where beauty is defined by what you wear and the way you look; and value is placed on what you do, where you live, and what you drive. From this superficial perspective, God peered into my soul and showed me that my identity is in Him alone. I began feeling the freedom from shaving, plucking, combing, styling, and makeup. I wondered to myself how many hours a week, a month, or a year the average woman spends trying to look beautiful to the world. I embraced the saying,

"Beauty comes from within." I began seeing the transformation of my physical body as miraculous. Not only did God show me this picture of myself but also His vision to see past the masks to the innermost part of our being: the heart. And if we seek His, we will find ours.

*God does not see the same way people see. People look at the outside of a person, but the Lord looks at the heart.*

-1 Samuel 16:7 (NIV)

# Your Story

## Your Story

# HAIR CARES

*And even the very hairs of your head are all numbered.*

-Matthew 10:30 (NIV)

I remember asking my friend about her hair loss from chemotherapy. She distinctly remembered the day clumps of her hair began falling out. She tried to get through the day at work without anyone noticing. All she wanted, or rather needed, was to get home. She told me she cried herself to sleep that night.

My story is a little different. I mentally tried to prepare myself for what was to happen with my hair, but honestly, how can you really? I cut my hair really short at first. I thought it would make the transition easier. I made an appointment with a cosmetologist who also fitted wigs for people in my situation. I decided to invite my daughter, my mom, my sister, and my niece along. I thought I would try to make it like an adventure, and I knew they would want to be included; anything at all they could do would help them feel useful. I know at times it was hard for them to watch me go through this, so making them a part of this day not only helped them, but it helped me turn what could have been a dreadful event into a fun and memorable experience.

When we got to the salon, a tall, grayish blonde woman in her sixties, if I had to guess, called me to the back of the room. She spoke with a Scottish accent. She was very dear yet stern. She let my family know, even my mom, that this day was not about them but about me and about making *me* happy. It took a little warming up, but my mom soon came around to seeing that this beautiful stranger was only trying to make me feel special and cared for. The first thing "Bobbi" did was give me a buzz cut. My hair was shedding quite a lot, and although I didn't expect it, I understood that it needed to be done. With that done, we began trying on wigs. My family took pictures as I tried on every color available. I found out I would never make it as a blonde and that my natural color was actually the best choice for me. The wig I chose was actually beautiful with different subtle highlights and lowlights. We ended the day from the fitting with a delicious dinner. Mom, ILo, Nicole, and Lindsay helped me face that day with an attitude defiant of the disease that was waging war on my mind and body.

About one week later, the little bit of hair I had left began falling out. I stopped at my sister's house on my way home from work. I asked her if she would help me. She didn't expect me to ask her for a sticky lint roller, and still I don't think she understood at first what my intentions were. I began to use it on my head, and it worked great! The hair made some really nice, swirled patterns on the sheets. I saved them. I thought I would send them to my mom, who had gone back home after spending the winter with us to help out. I decided not to put a return address on it and smiled as I imagined her opening this strange parcel. To this day, she still has those sticky sheets in her dresser drawer! We still had to use a razor to get everything, and then I put on the wig. We fussed with it and trimmed it a little here and there, but I couldn't get myself to wear it. I felt more self-conscious with the wig than just sporting the bald look and ball cap. Then, more than ever, I felt the shadow of the disease looming over me, and the fear, once again, began to creep in. I had to remind myself that I was "fearfully and wonderfully made" despite how I looked. I knew that this too shall pass and become a memory to which I would inspire, reflect, and draw strength from.

*I praise you because I am fearfully and wonderfully made; your works are wonderful, I know that full well.*

-Psalm 139:14 (NIV)

# Your Story

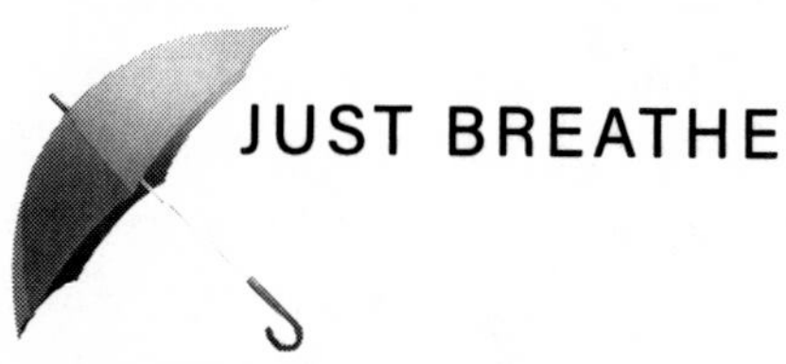

# JUST BREATHE

If you've ever had an anxiety attack, you know how frightening it can be. It's as if your mind and body are disconnected somehow. It's truly amazing how much stress we can endure, but there is a breaking point. For example, six weeks before my mastectomies, I was given so much information, paperwork, and tests that required nearly split-second decisions. These were life-altering decisions that one would usually take time to contemplate fully. I was taken off-guard, and my defenses were down. It felt like the weight of the world was on my shoulders. I wondered if I had made the right choices for myself. I was still trying to absorb all that was happening to me. I felt fine. I had no symptoms, yet I saw the X-rays, and even so, I had a hard time accepting these turns of events in my life. I was given all the options over and over and over again. I hoped I had picked the "right" doctors and surgeons to whose hands my life would be entrusted.

I realized the best way to mentally and physically prepare for this journey was to take it in steps. I couldn't look at the "big picture", only that which was right in front of me. When that was done, I would look to the next step. That's how it worked for me: one step at a time, one day at a time, one week at a time—no more. This way I left room (rather, margins or spaces) in my mind for whatever else life might throw at me.

So this was my life for one year and six months. Until I figured out how to compartmentalize this "stuff" in my brain, I would get what would seem like mini panic attacks. I think there was so much information and so many tests and appointments that my life suddenly turned into one big roller coaster. With lots of turns, pitfalls, screaming hills, and valleys, it made my head spin just to think of it.

Four weeks after my surgery, it was time to get back to work. I was driving and talking to my daughter on my cell phone. Suddenly, I had an overwhelming feeling that I wasn't ready. I thought to myself, *I can't do this. I'm not ready!* My palms were sweaty, and my heart raced. I started to cry. I had to pull over. I knew they were expecting me to work, but I wasn't ready to be seen yet. I wanted to crawl back under the sheets of my bed and shut the world out for another day.

I prayed, I went, I arrived, and I cried again. My welcome back was warm and consoling. They knew and were prepared to give what they could to help me ease back into my usual weekday routine. And then, to my surprise, came a delivery of flowers from my daughter. There was no name on the card, but I knew from whom it was sent. It read, "Just breathe," and "I love you." It warmed my heart, and it was just what I needed for someone to say. That was my "fix" for the day, and from that day on, I told myself over and over again, *I can do this, I am loved, and I am not alone.* So just breathe deeply as if God's breath were upon you, filling you with His senses and calming every nerve and beat of your heart. Then exhale, slowly, and feel the peace of Him who is.

*Again Jesus said, "Peace be with you! As the Father has sent me, I am sending you." And with that he breathed on them and said, "Receive the Holy Spirit."*

-John 20:21-22 (NIV)

# *Your Story*

# Your Story

# PASS IT ON

The Lord prepares us for the work He is doing. He involves us in His work to help others in need. While I was going through treatment for cancer, He was preparing me for something greater. At the time, I was mainly focused on getting through the day; I was focused on myself.

In Romans 8:28 (NIV), His Word says, "And we know that in all things God works for the good of those who love Him, who have been called according to His purpose." I've always loved this promise of hope. During times of despair, I would wonder and ask, *"Why me, Lord?"* Then I would think, *"Why not me?"* It's hard to think outside of yourself when you are the one in pain. It's like standing in the middle of a storm; the winds of fury are circling around you. It isn't until you get to the edge that you can see the ravaging effects and the vast display of its power.

During the storms of our lives, it is hard to understand why it is happening and the purpose behind it. What did I do to deserve this? What I have realized, however, is once we get through it and look back, the picture becomes clear. We start to see His blessings, His love, His protection, His provision, and His purpose. He is preparing you for something greater. It may be something you never could imagine yourself doing. However, when you allow God's hands to partner with yours, you will see His intentions become your reality. Sometimes, He makes us go through the storms in order to help others weather theirs. Who better to be called upon than someone who has already been through it? That storm in your life may be the loss of a loved one, or an unexpected illness. Whatever the circumstance, God is going to use it for His good. You may not see it at the time of your suffering, but once it has passed, a glimmer of God's work at hand becomes evident.

I have found there is camaraderie with others who have shared similar experiences. That common thread can create an instant bond with an otherwise perfect stranger. Whether you are just beginning your journey or have finished, God may place you in the middle of someone else's storm in order for you to help them. Your counsel, your understanding, and your testimony may be just what they need to shed a little hope and light in the darkness they are facing.

Let His purpose in you be the link you need to share with others what God has done. Then, when we pass it on, His blessings spill over into one another, and the links of His loving chain grow longer and stronger because we said, "We will," and we did.

*Whatever you have learned or received or heard from me, or seen in me—put it into practice. And the God of peace will be with you.*

-Philippians 4:9 (NIV)

# Your Story

# Your Story

# WHITE HORSES

*The Lord is my strength and my shield; my heart trusts in him, and I am helped. My heart leaps for joy and I will give thanks to him in song.*

-Psalm 28:7 (NIV)

When I think of a white horse, I picture a knight in shining armor coming to save the day. This fairytale image I once imagined as a child seems silly, yet deep down I think the kids in us all want to believe in heroes and Easter bunnies and Santa Claus. The joy, adventure, mystery, and the happily-ever-afters continue to live on as we share them time and time again with our children and grandchildren. Just the wonder and twinkle in their eyes helps to bring these fantasies to life in their imaginations.

As we grow older, however, reality skews the wonder and colorful images in our minds' eye. We believe only in that which can be explained, which undermines the innocence and the mystery of what we secretly long to hang onto. Faith, on the other hand, is believing in what you cannot see or understand and then letting God take control of the circumstance.

Whenever I am depressed, sick, or overwhelmed, I try to imagine happier times of days gone by. Many times, I recall the holiday seasons as a child, especially Christmas. In fact, I will listen to Christmas music in July if I am in need of a spiritual lift!

My toughest battle yet (and I am sure there will be more) was my diagnosis of breast cancer. Looking back over those eighteen months, I realize there were many battles being fought—some at the same time. There was the emotional battle; the fight to stay strong and the constant temptation to withdraw into myself. It was a battle of wills. I asked myself, "Do I let this blackness take control of me, or do I allow God to use this for something good"? I couldn't imagine what that would be then, but that is when I put my faith to the test and allowed God to show me Himself right in the midst of the war I was fighting. He gave me the determination and strength to carry on. And while He carried me in my struggle, He was blessing me in my suffering.

So, time and time again, I was rescued in the battle I was facing. My knight wasn't the prince I imagined as a child but now a soldier coming to save me from the darkness of despair and anguish and the ill effects of the poison now coursing through my veins—the "red devil" they called it. It was administered intravenously every three weeks over the course of several months. Amazingly, our veins are equipped to withstand this toxic waste that, ordinarily, causes third-degree burns on contact. It took six hours to administer the liquid used to make me as sick as possible without killing me, and each time, each hour, and each day, God would rescue me. He was and continues to be my knight in shining armor.

So when you are faced with a battle that seems insurmountable, "Put on the full armor of God...the belt of truth...the breastplate of righteousness...the shield of faith... the helmet of salvation and the sword of the Spirit, which is the Word of God,"(Ephesians 6:13-17, NIV) and let God rescue you from your infirmities.

*I saw heaven standing open and there before me was a white horse, whose rider is called Faithful and True. With justice he judges and makes war. His eyes are like blazing fire, and on his head are many crowns. He has a name written on him that no one knows but he himself. He is dressed in a robe dipped in blood, and his name is the Word of God. The armies of heaven were following him, riding on white horses and dressed in fine linen, white and clean.*

-Revelation 19:11-14 (NIV)

# Your Story

# EPILOGUE

I never would have imagined that God would use my experience as a witness to others in their suffering. All I know is, at the time of my diagnosis, I went looking for such a book as this in order to learn how to deal with the array of emotions this life-changing journey was presenting me.

Well, it has been seven years since the first edition of this book was published. A lot has happened. From the moment God told me to praise Him, I felt His hand at work in my life. He not only provided the spiritual needs to endure what I call my "walk in the valley", but He provided the love and support of my friends, and the community of believers from my home town and my church family to pray for me in my struggle. Even when I couldn't pray for myself, I always felt Him with me. Each day, it got easier and easier to give Him thanks for this season of my life. I am pleased to say that it has been over eleven years and I am still cancer free! Sometimes it feels like it is a distant memory and other times it feels like it was yesterday. Something or someone will trigger a memory and I find myself right back there in the storm. When I look back, however, I can see a bit clearer. He opened my eyes so I could see the positive things in the midst of the storm raging in and around me. God held me in the "eye" of that storm. Too many circumstances happened that could only be explained as God's intervention. Amazingly, I had no fear for my life. I knew that He would be with me, whether it would continue in this life or the next. The peace that God speaks of that surpasses all understanding is true. It is the only reason I can think of why, when I was face-to-face with my own mortality, I wasn't' afraid.

My only regret was that I didn't keep a journal from the very beginning. Daily occurrences happened where I could see God's activity through scripture, people, song or manifestations of His guiding hand. If I had to sum up in one word what the single most important thing I have learned through this experience, it would be perspective; perspective of God and life in general. We all know that no one is exempt from tragedy. However, it is how we handle those circumstances that set us apart. How do we move forward? Well, in Philippians 4:9 it says to put into practice that which we have seen or heard or received in Him. In other words, pay it forward! Your story may be just what someone else needs to hear that will bring the change they need that will make the difference. We are all God's instruments to be used for His glory. By putting what we know into action not only blesses us but magnifies His name. Something I strive to do every day is exchange my perception with God's perspective. This puts a whole new light on my circumstances when I choose to practice it. In a devotional by Pastor David Jeremiah, he wrote how "we see obstacles where God sees opportunities and we see predicaments where God sees providence." I can only imagine how different the world would be if everyone put this into practice.

Going through cancer changed me. It was the hardest thing I have ever been through and yet it was the most blessed. I grew more in my faith in those eighteen months than I had the previous twenty years since I invited Christ into my heart. There is a scripture in Job 42:5 that says, "I have heard of you by the hearing of the ear, but now my eye sees you". You see, Job loved God but it was only through adversity that he really got to "know" God in His true character. I feel the same. I loved God, yes, but our relationship was one-sided. I was definitely "in the world" so to speak. I went to church and I read my bible... sometimes. I didn't have the discipline or the yearning to seek God like I have today. But who I was then and who I am now I would not have become had I not gone through cancer. I can say that having cancer put me on a fast track to knowing Jesus like never before. It forced me to "look up" and realize that the time may come sooner than later that I will be face-to-face with my Creator. That was the turning point when my perspective of life began to change. Things became less and less important to me and family and friends became precious. Life became a gift to hold and give thanks for and more and more a thread of simplicity to life and the decisions on how I was redeeming my time here on earth took precedence. Less became more to me. I found that I could be happier with less so a season of "purging" of things in my life, including the downsizing of our home, followed. That scripture in Matthew 6:20 became real to me. It says: "For where your treasure is, there your heart will be also" (NKJV). It was very hard giving up some things but when I finally released it, a new sense of freedom came after. God was showing me how to let go of things I had a very tight grip on-some things I hadn't even realized until He showed me. I began to see that the things of this world are all temporary and have no lasting rewards. What really counts is eternal. I want to be sure when I stand before Jesus that I hear His words, "Well done, good and faithful servant"(Matt.25:21 NKJV).

Some of the things I did and would recommend to all who read this book are to pour yourself into His Word, especially the Psalms. Also, listen to soothing and uplifting Christian music, spend time in prayer with Him, offer up your thanksgiving and praise, and you will experience Him in a way you never have before. Jesus will anoint you with His Spirit, and you will know that "in all things God works for the good of those who love him who have been called according to his purpose," (Romans 8:28, NIV)

Someone once told me that "the views from the mountaintops are nice, but fruit is grown in the valleys". And it says in Romans 5:3-4: "knowing that tribulation produces perseverance; and perseverance, character; and character, hope." Now that doesn't mean we have to feel good about any trial we are put under, but God will use it for our good and His glory if we let Him. Just what He has started in me since the publication of this book is evidence of that. A few years ago I was invited to be part of a ministry called Heartfully Alive in which our primary mission is to set the kindling in people's hearts on fire through the work of the Holy Spirit. Also, I have been working on a devotional including "Letters from Heaven". God has been speaking these so-called "letters" into me for about six years now. They have been manna from heaven to me so I want to share them with you so you can be blessed. You will see at the end of this book I have included one of those letters; that which was shared at our last women's conference. It will be at the end of this book for you to read.

I pray that you will allow God to bless you in your journey. May you learn to praise Him in your suffering and feel the peace, love, and strength that only your Creator can provide. When this season of your life has passed, you too will be able to reflect on this time and see how the hand of God was preparing you for something greater all along.

I have made it known that speaking and writing was never on my "bucket list" of things to do in my lifetime. But as I have said before, when you "let go and let God", you will find that His intentions become your reality and your surrender becomes your victory. You see, when we give Him ourselves, He gives us Himself! Just think, the God of the Universe loves you! Even in the midst of darkness and despair, God sees our future and He holds out the best for us. He can turn our tragedies to triumph and our sorrows to blessings. He will carry you in your struggle and bless you in your suffering. So when we can't see where the journey takes us or how it is going to end, let us walk by faith. For some, that journey will become their legacy to be left behind for others. Theirs is the ultimate reward. However, on this side of Heaven there is always going to be trials and pain, but through it there are moments of triumph and growth. I hope those moments lead you into a deeper relationship with Him and that His reality for you will be the legacy you leave behind for others to glean upon.

*Do not be anxious about anything, but in everything, by prayer and petition, with thanksgiving, present your requests to God. And the peace of God, which transcends all understanding, will guard your hearts and your minds in Christ Jesus.*

-Philippians 4:6-7 (NIV)

# "LETTER FROM HEAVEN"

*Dearly Beloved,*

I am calling you upward and outward--upwards to me, the God-head, and outwards to reach beyond borders. My reach is unreachable. I want you to imagine it. Believe in the unbelievable, the unimaginable, and the impossible, for nothing is beyond Me. I want you to embrace the idea because my power with all my love lives in your heart. I love getting to know you. I've known you from the beginning of time but you are now letting me into the innermost recesses of your heart where your true beauty lies. It's always been there. As you have been steadily seeking to know my heart, yours is being unveiled as well. You are beginning to see the beauty among the ashes. You are becoming what I have created you to be in Me. You are my heart, my love, and my masterpiece. I want you to begin to see yourself through the eyes of your Creator. As you begin to believe in the transformation you can move into action! As you capture this portrait in your mind's eye, let it also be captured in your heart; for that is where I live through my Holy Spirit. He is your guide, your teacher, and your advocate. I will be stretching the boundaries of your heart because I want you to reach beyond yourself to others whose hearts are waiting to be transformed. It is within you and within all of my children the yearning to know Me, their true Father. I created the heart and I eagerly await its invitation; for it is in the invitation that leads to transformation that leads my children to their rightful heart and home—it leads to Me.

# A SALVATION PRAYER

*Lord Jesus,*

I want to know you personally. Thank you for dying on the cross for my sins. I receive you into my heart as my Lord and Savior. Thank you for forgiving my sins and giving me eternal life. Take control of the throne of my life and make me the kind of person you want me to be. In Jesus Name, I pray.

Amen.

CPSIA information can be obtained
at www.ICGtesting.com
Printed in the USA
FFOW02n1151170618
47135732-49692FF

9 781640 452930